Sympathetic Systems

Sympathetic Systems

poems by

Carole Simmons Oles

Lynx House Press
Spokane, Washington
2000

Cover painting *Augustine Roulin with Baby* by Vincent Van Gogh has
been reprinted with the permission of
The Metropolitan Museum of Art, New York

Design by Christine Holbert

Library of Congress Cataloging-in-Publication Data
Oles, Carole Simmons
Sympathetic systems: poems / by Carole Simmons Oles.
p.   cm.
ISBN 0-89924-104-2 (PAPER)
1. Women—Family relationships—Poetry.
2. Loss (Psychology)—Poetry.
I. Title
PS3565.L43 S96 2000
811'.54—dc21

ACKNOWLEDGMENTS

Poems contained in this volume originally appeared in the following journals:

Alaska Quarterly: "Beginning and Ending with Mahler's *Kindertotenlieder*," "Definition: Northern California Autumn"

Articulations: The Body and Illness in Poetry: "Father's Fall"

Atlanta Review: "At the Races with Jan"

The Boston Phoenix: "The Odds and My Mother"

Colorado Review: "Echo Cardiogram"

The Cream City Review: "Visiting My Formerly Runaway Daughter and Her Husband at the Orchard in Vermont"

Denver Quarterly: "At Nightfall in Vermont"

Emrys Journal: "How I Sang: A Reclamation"

Field: "Victory"

I've Always Meant to Tell You: Letters to Our Mothers, An Anthology of Women Writers: "Running Away with Ralph"

Kalliope: "The Mammogram"

The Kenyon Review: "Voices: Mother and Daughter"

Nimrod: "Women Near Sea"

Poetry Miscellany: "We Part the Waves on Main Street"

Poetry Northwest: "The Finger"

Prairie Schooner: "Evolution Dream," "Sleeping Daughter," "Summer, the City," "The Unfinished Gallery"

Stunts: "Action," "Little Sister, Her Flight"

TriQuarterly: "To A Daughter at Fourteen, Forsaking the Violin"

Watershed: "Old Wars," "Pneumonia/Delirium"

The Women's Review of Books: "Questions of Fashion: The Fifties."

The Loneliness Factor
Quarry
Night Watches: Inventions on the Life of Maria Mitchell
The Deed
Stunts

CONTENTS

A funny little girl.
How could she have known
that even despair yields profit
if by some good fortune
one should live a little longer.

—Wislawa Szymborska, from "Laughter"

Manic depression, mood swings of depression and euphoria that afflict more than 3 million Americans, often takes years to diagnose.

A sample of 500 patients reported that it took an average of eight years to get the correct diagnosis. Because the disorder begins most commonly between ages 15 to 19, an untreated case disrupts a person's life at a vulnerable time, possibly leading to drug abuse and failure in college and on the job.

Recovery can occur whether the disorder is viewed as biological or not.

—from Newsletters of the Alliance for the Mentally Ill of Vermont, 1995

For Julie
and in memory of Helen

HOW I SANG: A RECLAMATION

Company sat at the porcelain table drinking coffee, laughing
at jokes while I hunched cross-legged underneath and looked
right up dresses to a lace edge of slip, a flash of garter
on thigh. Leaning back, I waited for Daddy's announcement, then
licked my lips, swallowed hard and began his favorite
elegiac number, laboring up to the sharp high *light* of

"Just a Song at Twilight." They clapped, so as an
encore I did "Don't Fence Me In" there in our three-room
apartment. Cottonwood trees? On our street
no trees but the one-branched street lamps, Halloween gibbets.

So why was I singing? Fierce to be heard and not seen
I got the rule wrong, got disembodied too soon.
My parents called me a song whose words were all planned.
Mostly our family didn't sing—not even my aunt the near
Opera Star, shut up by her father's *I forbid* . . .
Nobody knew any better then; the people were ignorant.
Some of them, later, whistled away their own names.

THE ODDS AND MY MOTHER

If she had stayed at the third-floor window one second longer
pinning that corner of sheet to the clothesline
she wouldn't have seen a man walk on the moon
or helped my father to let go of the earth.

Just pulling her head in, *Oh* she heard called
at her as the laundry with a woman inside
it accelerated down three stories more
to the courtyard and hit like a bowling ball in a tub.

My mother told me later her guardian angel
had been near her, and who am I to say different?
I was ten, I fell fast asleep that night on sheets
that still smelled of sun and a breeze off the river.

FATHER'S FALL

The hospital lights punish my eyes.
A doctor is scolding me for not
considering my mother who does not
seem to have this problem
swallowing, keeping hiccups back,
keeping her dress dry. I will not
go upstairs to see him the doctor says,
I will sit here and stop it.

The police say he rolled
down the subway stairs. Blood
nests in his head like bad birds.
Upstairs they cut out
the crows. Something about
arithmetic, 50 and 50.

How could my daredevil father,
washer of Empire State windows,
91st floor, fall down 22 steps?

I think of the baby glass
in the kitchen. Afternoons
would fall into nights and his words
spin onto the table like aggies
until he could hardly
stand up to lie down.

3

Tonight, on the waiting-room couch
I lie in myself, awake and little.
What if he dies here,
how will I get what I need? —
hating my piggy heart.

THE FINGER

When Rose Damiano slammed
the door to Apartment 2A
on my mother's finger
she gave only a gasp, and blood—
slow at first, as if roused from a nap,
then running like a prisoner set free
from her smashed middle finger.
I watched fairytale red
paint the porcelain tiles.

Dumbhead Rosie! why didn't she look
what she was doing, why
didn't she close their door
on her own mother's finger?

My mother always knew what to do.
She threw ice in a towel,
wrapped her hand
like a baby in bunting.
We walked the block
to the nearest doctor, a fat man
in stained vest and slobbery lips.
My mother sat still for that stinging
needle of mercy before he inflicted
black thread to hold her pulse in.

Now, decades later, I want
to ask the Godhead
who speaks not my language

Haven't you and Rose Damiano
done enough to this woman?

whose heart they say needs a door
a valve cut from pig gut or plastic.
In their mouths it sounds small.
Maybe the size of a thimble.

BEGINNING AND ENDING WITH MAHLER'S KINDERTOTENLIEDER

for Gary, September 14-21, 1947

Look at us well, for soon we will be far away.

Eyes closed, hypothetical blue.
Red hair, silk threads woven into a cap
across the fontanelle
that wouldn't need to grow hard.
Tiny fingers arranged at your sides
on the white cover, nails perfect abalone.

A 'blue baby' they said
but your skin looked pink to me.
Was it makeup? the same disguise
I've seen on aunts and uncles,
on our father. *Our.*

I never saw you breathe
but I watched you traverse
the globe of our mother's belly,
placed my hand on your tour.
I didn't look well enough
to last this half-century.

Two years later, they could do the Blalock procedure
and fix the traitor valve.
Our sister never saw you even once.
I befriend men named Gary.

Live infants sleep with their hands up
as if, about to be robbed, they surrender.

You've taken a walk to the hills over there, merely gone ahead.

SUMMER, THE CITY

The crazy lady, we called her
in her dusty black dress sitting
at the street corner just where
the drain opened up like a leer.

Crazy because she split
her legs to the world: no Lollipop briefs,
a black thatch she didn't
even know to keep veiled.

Hours she stayed talking to air
When her mouth flapped we could see
her gums chew the sounds
those thin arms conducted.

We didn't ask our parents where she lived
or why nobody led her back home.
On roller skates we drew circles—

she was the cheese who stands alone,
some foreign, stinking kind—
and we had to grow into women.
Under hair like used batting,
pale as our baby sister's her scalp shone.

SENT FOR DADDY'S EVENING STAR

The man behind Coke bottle eyeglasses whispered Hiya, Honey.
Mother had issued the don'ts, her index finger a gavel.
Run, I thought out loud. *Bad girl,*
the rabbit in my chest banged at her organdy blouse.
I wanted my sweater, my room.

RAPE COUNSELING, THE 60s

You
French horn player, physicist grad student
from the Bronx, blind date
set up by the Psych major
who hadn't psyched you out,

after you picked me up
in a Triumph we drove
to your apartment on Etna
where you cooked spaghetti,
then exposed the sofa bed.
I looked for the fire escape—*none*—
but you'd been in training.
I had my flimsy negatives
and a waist I'd been taught
to keep small. If I told you
clearly enough you'd have to
give up your claim to my clothes.
What were you doing?
This happened in alleys, not
on Simmons sofa beds
that smelled of home, not
with classical music-playing
formula-cracking men with degrees.

At the Health Center, the woman psychiatrist
let me talk about
what I had
let happen

then she bore her gray eyes behind glass into me
"Well . . . you're not exactly Marilyn Monroe . . ."
a verdict I'm still deconstructing.

That was the one time I saw her.
I spent the rest of the year
meeting minds with George Herbert:
trusting men metaphysical, dead.

AT THE RACES WITH JAN

Sligo, Ireland, anniversary of our father's death

Here 6-year-olds read the forms,
place bets, and win.
Serious as bankers, they argue odds
and head for candy racks outside
the quonset hut where we sip stout.

It's you we carry in our eyes, you
our gambling father who used to
phone illegal bets to Rudy
the man with no last name,

you who sees the pack and one
horse edging through, the jockey
yelling, whipping as you'd say
to beat the band,

into the last furlong—
the ground shakes in our spines,
sun pokes over clouds then slips
behind Ben Bulben as for you

Henry Reginald out of O'Reilly
our pick Kilgarvin
noses first across the line.

QUESTIONS OF FASHION: THE FIFTIES

Like fawns parted from the doe
in hunting season, we mostly tried
not to crunch the dead leaves, not to parade
our scent. But who

put us into those blouses
you could see just about
everything through, with sedate
Peter Pan collars to raise

a sense of irony? The buds
of our breasts hid in 'training bras'—
for what athletics we weren't sure.
We stepped into the irons of a fad.

Nylon on each female torso
in geometry class, like the cellophane wrap
around lollipops, or the seventh, last
veil. How could mothers allow

such displays to leave home?
The only one of us worth watching
was Lorraine, who moved oiled, like a cat
to the board to do problems.

She was one. While we danced to 'Blue Tango'
with boys whose heads nicked our nipples,
whose breath smelled like Clearasil,
she was 'stayin' out late' with Johnny Ray.

And while we bared our sex
above, Dark Continents below kept densely
swathed in layers of lingerie.
In Hygiene, we read a vacuumed text.

But how could girls solve
theorems, stripped to the waist?
I failed every test.
House was the given I proved.

ECHO CARDIOGRAM

1

Smeared with lubricant, my chest prepares
for futuristic loving from this mike
whose cord's attached to the man-tall machine
that stares me down from a blank TV face.
Our go-between, the nurse, massages cold
above my heart and throws the switch on transport.
I came here to head off trouble at the pass.

2

As big as your fist, they say, but what I see
—this captive glob—would shrink from fight,
would hide in corners hoping no one spoke.
I want my clothes, I want my self back.
The Moslems know that cameras steal souls.
A Mayan sacrifice, my heart sticks tight
inside the metal man to make him thrive.

3

I've studied physics, know a thing exists
in one place at a time. Ergo I'd deny
my heart resides in me and out . . . yet
I survive to watch the transplant.
Look too hard and everything will stop
so I look slant: butterfly wings open
and close, a sea anemone contracts.

4

Though I seem heartless, my heart's guide has two:
the nurse is pregnant. If I turn the microphone
on her, what size will that fish-heart be—
an olive, a peach pit, the pupil of an eye?
Transparent, and like my almost brother's
without the flaw. Some machinery might
have saved him. But for Vietnam, or dope?

5

The charts surround me, saying textbook stuff,
aortic stenosis, ventricular fibrillation—
Science and Latin articulating griefs.
Hearts preserved on film bear witness
how we sponge life up, from appetite to loss
and back. When lightning bridges arc
between black cliffs I cross, and cross.

REPTILIAN

Six months man and wife,
they posed in a white orchard,
heads turned to each other
like blossoms toward the sun.
She wore a navy blue dress,
brass buttons marched down
from her throat, out of the frame
which neatly cut her
at the waist. On the other
side of the camera, his mother
composed them that way.
The camera opened a keyhole
between them and her eye.
Bees zeroed in as they smiled,
sure of themselves, eye to eye.
Snow blossoms swirled,
mown hay sweetened.
They would be fixed,
glossed on that paper for years
before crawling away—
and blood so cold.

ACTION

At 3:40 A.M. each empty bedroom glows
with cold street light as room to room
I check on the aura of children
waking with fever, crowing
the raucous cry of croup
before I sweep them into the steamy shower,
into the Emergency Room.

Emergency! I can't find those children.
Lives, impedimenta spread across continents
like the products of a midair collision.
Who watched from the tower that course?

Today I stand in one of the bedrooms with my mother,
turning the dials on my voice to get the right
mix for the sentence in which I say
                                                    divorce

and later I remember her story,
how one starvation season her father left the farm
to work as a lumberjack in Minnesota.
That winter the stovepipe caught fire
and her mother, Henrietta Wittenbrink Kampmeyer,
grabbed the red column in her bare hands,
ripped it off and threw it hard
into the snow.

PEN MAN SHIP

She could feel the heat off his red face
as her father's brows joined to frown
upon her wrongly held pen.
Her shaky scrawl—the letters not
sufficiently round; loose-jointed,
rickety—sloped below to
escape the policing blue line,
or climbed to beat through that sky.

At school, the Rosenhaus method taught
each letter identically formed
by thirty sweating hands while the pens
scraped and spat on white,
while the inkwells dried and clotted, needed
stirring like the blood of an old idea.
Miss Covell strode up and down the rows
pronouncing judgment on their names.
When ever would the recess bell ring,
the huge windows open like sails?

Once, her father had the answer.
In third grade, from the front seat
where his teacher could watch him
he shot his hand up, forgot
the pen he wielded, and the teacher
donned before all a polka dot middy
with face to match. That ink
he recited even unto the day
his hand stumbled across white space.

Now the daughter learns his name again,
raises it from the dead to patrol
between her and the one she's unwed.
No man leans over her pen saying *dot it,*
round it, make it flow, unperturbed.
She writes, pressing hard
her new old name rigged with
two snakeskins, one self, humming, praise.

TO A DAUGHTER AT FOURTEEN, FORSAKING THE VIOLIN

All year, Mozart went under
the sea of rock punk reggae
that crashed into your room every
night and wouldn't recede however
I sandbagged our shore
and swore to keep the house dry.
Your first violin, that halfsize
rented model, slipped out of tune
as you played Bach by ear
Suzuki method with forty other virtuosos
who couldn't tie their shoes.
Then such progress: your own
fiddle, the trellised notes you read,
recitals where I sat on hard chairs.
Your playing made me the kid.
If I had those fingers! . . .
Five of yours grasped my pinky,
the world before you grew teeth.
Okay. They're your fingers.
To paint the nails of, put rings on,
hold cigarettes in, make obscene
gestures or farewells with.

WE PART THE WAVES ON MAIN STREET

She in her dayglo orange crewcut
I, dun in all critical cover
save reflected glory that her hues emit.
Are we the same tribe, I and this womanling

the Pfc. wearing what used to be
designer pants, one incarnation ago dyed flu green
later reborn handpainted between wide stripes
a permanent marking of runes hieroglyphics
slogans that march over the difficult terrain
of her nevermore Mama's little baby's bum

which in the steamroom of July
beside a window overlooking towers of learning
the o.b. summoned (his partner's weekend on the Cape)
and while a radiance of neurons yelled URGENT
along my inner thighs, unready, resisting she
answered, finally, the hormones of convenience
and was born.

She the brother pronounced *dolly* wouldn't
lie still, go away, be merely pretty she who
now when the Pontiac slows down
and the all-American sticks his head out
confirming her opinions of the white man
to hoot *Ay freak, I like yuh haihcut*
and the spear sticks in my rib yet she endures
dear brave, most lonely dancer at full moon.

I drum her home.

VISITING MY FORMERLY RUNAWAY DAUGHTER AND HER HUSBAND AT THE ORCHARD IN VERMONT

> *Let's drink to the hard-working people;*
> *Let's drink to the salt of the earth.*
> —*The Rolling Stones*

I need to explain to myself, so I tell my friends
you've dropped out of the middle class after one
short generation—mine, which rose on the spines
of workingclass parents. Out of their neighborhoods,
their tax brackets, their broken English.

When I arrive up the dirt road, having stopped
for more detailed directions at the orchard
packing house, and having made nonetheless
one wrong turn, one stop at the wrong white
house, you are waiting. For me, and for
him, your husband two hours overdue, gone fishing.
Oh daughter of the strong arm and sunburned nose.
Oh child of my disorderly bosom.
I am glad to sit at your sticky table,
glad to drink the strong coffee you've brewed,
you remember my addiction.

We hear an engine panting uphill and then he
and his fishing mate, Larry from Florida,
reel into the kitchen, bravely displaying one
8-inch fish of unknown origin. Larry is happy,

and your man heavy-lidded—maybe there has been beer—
and when Larry smiles and speaks, his top teeth wag.
I can't understand more than one word in his ten
but his smile says fine, and I shake his hand
as calloused as my stone-carving, window-cleaning,
metal-lathing father's. Your Bobby gets Larry
to clean the fish, to show him how, and when
the dirty job is done—we three have turned
squeamish from the lesson—Bobby wraps
the fish in the daily newspaper
and throws it into the freezer, where intaglio
stories of x's drunk-driving charge, y's
nine-pound boy, will solidify on its flank.

More coffee, Larry's departure, and a plan:
a tour of the orchard, the hidden sauna, the stream
then blueberry picking. But first
a snack of blueberries you two
have already gathered, set like sapphires
in vanilla yogurt unintentionally frozen. Delicious,
delicious, and you, child, by my side.

We stalk the rows of blueberry bushes, finding
what remains this late. The knock each globe
makes against cardboard reminds me of Sal's pail
in her story we read, heads touching over the page.
So many berries left, I am amazed
as we three spread out, calling to each other
from our separate camouflaging rows of green.
So many, and some so fat I can't believe
birds overlooked them, can't resist eating
them under the sun, under the pure blue of our reunion.

We combine our pickings—one luscious load—
and drive back to the bunkhouse.

The two Bartlett pears on your windowsill
lean onto each other's shoulders like lovers.
They are almost ready, one is blushing, the light
forms an aura around them. One stands straighter,
seems to hold the other up more, but may
need the other's leaning to have it seem so.

With dinner at the Jade Wah, we cannot
drink water because the supply is ruined
by industry. We wonder about the ice
in our soft drinks. I tell you of dark figures
squatting in ditches along the road from the airport
into the city of Calcutta; of your father fainting
on the bathroom tiles. . .Your father—
we blink once and pass him.
Last time we ate here, two summers ago, you
were living in a shack with six other people
and came to dinner barefoot. The management never flinched.

We reject our fortunes, rush down the highway
to the cinema to see "Parenthood." You sit between us
holding hands with Bobby and me, as onscreen
families sandpaper each other. One daughter
wears your name, and elopes. Her parents are
divorced; the father, a dentist, loves his hand on the drill.
Neither of us is conned by the ending: a baby
for each happy pair. Retrograde, we agree.

Back in the bunkhouse, your boss and two other pickers
sit at the kitchen table and kibbitz.
Paul has just returned from 3 months on a fishing boat
off the Aleutians and Terri, who smiles like a horizon,
follows crops across the continent.
Your boss says I look like your older sister.
I squirm when he jokes about elopement, cigarette breaks.
Soon it's bedtime—early. Work starts in the coolest
morning hours. You've made me a place upstairs:
a mattress on a boxspring on the floor. Across the hall,
you and Bobby will watch from your bed
sunrise over Monadnock. From my corner I see the shapes
of apple trees beyond the glass, silvered. I sleep.

By 5:30 the pans are rattling. Bobby cooks
blueberry pancakes so full of berries they clump
in the pan. He complains. I enjoy them. Good, strong
coffee and if I didn't have to leave, I'd stay,
try to pick apples. I don't want this to end now,
as I hug my girl and her husband.
I don't want them all to pile into the free,
battered Ford Fiesta, to follow them down
the rutted hill, out to the stop sign
she drives toward too fast,
to the packing house where they turn left
to get their orders for the day,
where she waves her hand out the window, her hand
toward which I, continuing straight, wave mine.

VOICES: MOTHER AND DAUGHTER

Except you lived, nothing was holy
that All-Hallows Eve, you my only
girl across an ocean and in a low
land where church bells spoke riddles.
Nothing holy about your bicycle
leaving the dark, colliding with his car.
Except you lived. Bless the dead martyrs,
your quick flesh and neurons, muscle and bone.

I believe nothing. Each telephone-you
contradicts the one before. Who
have you become? So you slid from me
pressing a forecast down my thigh.
Still your petals keep falling. What eye
centers your storm? They've drained the blood
clot from your brain, pronounced you healed,
loosed you to toy streets, real traffic.

While I travel north for Thanksgiving,
strangers watch your blood pressure hang
off the dial. I eat salmon, know nothing.
Returned home, I listen to voices harrow
my answering machine: you're gone. My own
voice batters back—Embassy, Consulate—
travelling in lines, cables. Faxes blurt petals
to a civil servant's desk—the recent photo—

eyes closed, you hold a pink bouquet.

You're finally found at hospital number two
where police deposited you unkempt and rhyming,
where doctors called you by another woman's
name, gave you her saving methadone
and nearly killed my shaggy girl again.
Meanwhile: I walk I talk I turn
the wheels of the diurnal: ball-bearing

smiles, piston legs, lens focussed on one hair.
          Interlude, Land's End, Indian Summer. . .
          At water's edge, alone, you cross your arms
          behind your back, a feather in each hand
          you stare out where seagulls swoop and haw. . .
          Once, you considered a chicken wing on your plate,
          lifted it to tender a last flap, and wouldn't eat.
I wake at five to phone from dark to light.

No one, no state or country, knows what
to do. At last the doctor says REPATRIATE.
You fly across the ocean with a nurse
but this won't bring you home. *Everything hurts*
you say long-distance and I hear your need
for hospital number three. *In the dream I have no key*
we trudge a city's streets, you're barefoot
till you find the one black boot.

Stop, please stop. But unstoppable, the scenes
repeat in summer when you bicycle to me
two hundred miles in two days
no sleeping bag, no clothes, no food,
no sunscreen. Having slept in fields,
drunk only water. Your shoulders flame

29

against white sheets on which I lay you down.
Don't I hear the voices? We're alone.

★

Looking for voices in the brain, new research
has tracked the blood flow that reflects
the jitter dance of nerves in those who hear
directives from their own speech-center hives.
(The same that hum when we speak silently to us.)
New research has also found the rind of brain
empathic with the limbic system, which rules emotions,
honors its fluent partner and dances tête-à-tête.
.

★

We're alone, but the voices say you're bad
and you know what you have to do. God,
what I have to do is get you to Emergency
an hour away. Just let's drive, I urge
not knowing how one minute will lead
into the next. You don't seem threatening
to anyone but you. I'm flying blind,
on love, on green hills that fall and rise

predictably. Cut clover soothes. Breathe
deeply, shining daughter, for this journey
               we've begun.

THE UNFINISHED GALLERY

The woman who speaks for three weeks in rhyme.
    Uncle Wiggly/ higgly-piggly/
    The horse/ that changed its course/
    Boom/ I fell in a waiting womb/
    Do you believe?/ Then you never have to grieve./
It must be funny—chops of laughter form her caesurae.
Like at parties the final martini sends someone out swinging,
one limb to the other of language, hundreds of feet
above ground, no one can stop him, they call up to
come down this instant before you get hurt
but these branches stretch infinite handshakes,
he can go on forever, up here, closer to light.

The woman who stares at her hands.
Because that gang of fir trees—ha! *Balm of Gilead*—
keeps whispering about animals she is
she draws the drapes, insists the window stay shut.
Because some chemical twangs the strings
to her legs they keep vibrating
a monotone, how to still them: start walking,
not stop, because the provinces of her body
speak separate dialects, only supreme
concentration may make them all sing
one national anthem, because
her hands used to make things: statues and masks,
beans vinaigrette—and now they hold
ghost towns, she stares at them as if

they're a photo of some long-lost relative
and if she stares long enough she'll remember the name.

The woman who won't take off her hat.
As if she hides something unorthodox:
a bird sitting on a pale lilac egg,
a plot to take over, a horn or transformer
that pokes through the tangle of chestnut.
Or another self, diminutive, cowering
who without provocation throws
off her clothes, flails at the sunlight
screaming curses at the hat, the head
her residence, the whole dressed world
with its fingers and teeth pointing at her.

The woman whose blow to the head helped her hearing.
Now she gets signals too high for the rest.
Now the microphone in her ear can't be switched off,
the voices more frequent than birdsong, traffic,
waterfalls, lullabies. The voices circle
and taunt her, they point to her soft parts,
they call her diseases, they dare her
to enter the flames and when she has risen
they chide her. They raise the army
that issues the weapons. They cloud like gnats
urging she must be swatted—use her hand
or the cranberry juice bottle.
You don't hear them? Just she, then, and dogs.

The woman who smiles like an elevator shaft,
luring you in so she can take you
where she wants to go. Her lips slide

like mechanical doors—no one's rung
for this transit—the rest of her features
stay steel. Her own mother wouldn't
recognize this smile. Her white baseball cap
backwards sends bulletins in black
magic marker. The woman who reads them
fills in forms, sits at the wheel.
She wants her to comb that hair,
stroll by the water, admire the view.
To eat solids, paint pictures, write letters,
grow her smiles upward from wiggling toes.
Wants her to come home on the range.

II. Before Release

The view was ours but we didn't own the field.
We belonged to each other, profiles told

how my cells swarmed in you, equally unbidden.
You'd signed yourself out for the afternoon

to watch with me perfect ideas float
in the August blue while close as we sat,

tight as our arms shawled each other's thin
shoulders, salt flavored the day. And only one

tissue between us, two torn ragged halves.
But we could breathe. Metal staves

burst and we breathed. Then it was late
. . . time to go back to our separate quiets . . .
you fed me sweet purple clover, and I ate.

III. Released, Going Away

You won't eat, day after day
only Diet Pepsi, decaf, tea.
How far can you retreat inside clothes
before they fall in a heap, nothing to hold
them upright and dancing like the ballerina
Shearer in those killing red shoes.
Where are you going? curves, pounds of you
burning off to fog I can't see through.

At your fifth birthday party we snapped
a photo, you and Jenny from the back:
round darlings in pigtails, arms circling
each other's waists, touch making words
between you, and Jenny who never spoke.
I mean *never.*
                    Could you hear her think?

IV. Rock

My mind, spoiled brat, wants reasons,
order, the eureka that helps humans
feel like Atlas not Prometheus.
It's all in our relationship to rock.

I'm the god who swept the kitchen floor,
who read the theories, broke her molars
grinding rock to comfort
cradling her child on muggy afternoons,

she who'd know at 12 to paint her face, one side
white, the other blue. The latest "meds"

would have to rock her if she'd take them.
Each child lifts the world to which she's chained.

V. Bracelet Thoughts

With these I circle you, arms
like Wonder Woman's silver cuffs
linking to repulse all harm.
I want to fasten you together
where you sprawl, wrist bent,
holding up black words on paper.
I want to sing you standing.
Such as when you played the violin
your bowing arm raised high, no break
at crucial wrist where notes would turn
to music. Such as when you called
me, small hand cupped around the words,
on your wrist roses engraved in gold
that slipped you in the nursery school
sandbox. Later to be replaced with vines
you'd ink there, impossible to lose.
What else got lost, went wrong?
Did someone hold too tight or not enough,
some larger will drag yours, dislocate song?
I know we formed a brace. Here's proof:
once I wore a plastic bracelet among
sterile halls. Yours on the ankle paired us
so lately two breaths in one lung.
Now faroff you wear a hospital I.D., alone.
And I'm just woman
wondering where they put it, because
the bandages ... the wounds ...

VI. RE-RUN

Last night I gave birth to
my daughter again
my Indian princess
I'd called her the first time
her robust bronze skin
the banner of jaundice—
now again she shone
rose gold as she entered
dream's delivery room
and with no slap began
to breathe.
               Long, she's long
I said to the doctor
the other woman
who read the scant measure
—eleven inches—
as my baby asked me
was the doctor her mom.
I am, come start to nurse
but she slipped into dark
leaving me with that
throb to be emptied.

COMPOSTING

Oak leaves, top layer, curly and crisp
crowned with peels, stems, rinds, pips—
the parts we couldn't eat. Heave them
up and over, bring the dark reformed
to sun, hose it all, stew it, soon
to be fed back to the garden, folded in.
First pick the remnant green globes
to pray for change on the East-facing sill,
the silk purple wands to rest horizontal.
Later spread the black, renewing daubs
that urge the next year's crop. *Year?*—one
day, then one, another, one again—
like runners radiating, holding sure
the only plant where strawberries can bear.

SYMPATHETIC SYSTEMS

I. December, A Continent Away

From gold country U.S.A. tonight I sail myself
toward the Dutch glottal lowlands
on an oceanliner, totter down passageways
of white stark rooms. In one my stricken
girl lies in a cardboard box the size
four pounds of shrimp are packed in, stilled
in ice, but I can't find that room, that box,
that my baby girl.

II. Flying to Connecticut in Spring

Between a snoring man in polyester
sweatsuit, wristwatch with three gold dials
and an adolescent boy recovering
from flu and skin eruptions, I strain

to see Lake Tahoe's green, the Sierra
flash such jewels I have to close my eyes,

surface old-time milk bottles, white
paper caps embraced by silver wire—
girlhood's play rings—and my father's fingers
blunt, too thick for handling cracked things.

Where you, child, stare in silence, thinning
I want to be warm milk,

encircle you, feel with all my fingertips'
receptors, sand the top layer off

to crack your code, and not scratch you.

III. After the Helpless Visit, Summer in Vermont

When nothing goes in or comes out from that mouth
when the new purple dress is already too big
the hair builds a nest of tongue-twisters
the feet follow each other like lemmings
when the case worker is 'non-coercive'
the case worker is on vacation
when all places are filled and summer is ending
when the medicine produces rigor
when the medicine causes trips and falls
when beside the knife-throwing lake
beside the tanned young rollerbladers
beside the sailboats   she is becalmed
when the trellises of generations collapse

then I dream my garden more lavish
—all plants, no lawn—
an avenue strewn
with green bean carpets
in their weave, green
bean-sized worms twitch
and all the buckets
hold cut
flowers going brown

IV. Sunday Afternoon, Temporary Respite

It could be any teenager's room, from the open window
hard rock blaring over neighbors' yards.
Here two days, you've washed your hair,
made a choice, said some words.
At the waterfront where we walked
you pointed out the Coast Guard.
I wanted to slap store clerks who stared.
Next door a man works under a blue pickup.
Here, all's green, the outpatients' garden
of lettuce, peas, cucumbers, squash.
Two men come out to smoke—one won't stop
talking, the other won't start.
Now the mechanic needs to weld;
nearby a woman plants a tree.
Sparks fly under the jacked-up truck:
hard rain on tin, then blue-white, hotter.
Shadows stretch, two metal lawn chairs
face each other, promising.
Bees float down. A horn blows—someone
in a hurry. But not in this
oasis. Here, time lulls.

V. More Respite: from The Pillow Book of Sei Shonogon Tenth Century, Heian Court, Japan

In summer the nights. Not only when the
moon shines, but on dark nights too, as
the fireflies flit to and fro, and even when
it rains, how beautiful it is!. . .
During the hot months, it is a great delight

to sit on the veranda, enjoying the cool of
the evening and observing the outlines
of objects gradually become blurred.

VI. SOON LEAVING, A FITFUL SLEEP

in which aloft I'm looking down
at several figures on shore arguing
and I scan left into endless waters
—no horizon—to a person either
swimming or in some frail boat alone
shrinking as I watch, a thin
purple voice reaches up, maybe singing.

REUNION, IN ORANGE

The same hat you wore during your frozen year.
We meet at the Candlelight Motor Inn
both in transit, one east, one west.
I'm on the public phone beside the parking lot
asking your grandmother if you've called
when I see—I think I see—your red van

but I've forgotten the front end of the van
is white, so when I tell her 'Bye, you're
here, I'm not sure it's you. I call
your name as the van passes—leaving me in
public waving to air, to the blank slot
between two trees where you, I thought, headed west

toward me this first day of the year in west-
ern Massachusetts, home state now van-
ished from us except for flyovers, allot-
ments to keep us warm and dry. Still, I'm yours.
And it *is* you, wearing the same orange hat as last Christmas in
the photo of us freezing beside the lake where I called

you and no one answered, only vapor dispersing. Called
myself the mother of sorrow riding west-
ward. But this singular day you're really in
the world: talking out, back; driving slick roads in your van,
bringing gifts you've bought or made. The best: your
standing in slush under a crisp white sky, no blot

just the writing of an ambitious script, a new plot
for your life. Once, you called
orange the color of madness. (You'd read Psych texts that year.)
Now, seeing you whole in orange, color of the west,
color of your hat, I want you to van-
quish all forces lined up outside and in,

witherers of that brilliant poppy of in-
estimable worth, that flowering polyglot
you are. To use your advantage: parts of the story of Van
Gogh; the flexible voice of Call-
iope to sing another epic west-
ern struggle—humanity's to be 'sane.' Your

years I invest hereby with love
and call them by your name alone.
You are your pilot, driving home your van.

THE DANGER ZONE GAME

Standing on the one leg of hope,
arms out for balance, shaky, I try
not to fall down. Do I see what I see?—
or; will it be there if I turn,
make one umbrella step?—*May I?*
No, you may not.

Your giant steps might make you super.
The man on the moon wouldn't scrap ground control.
Take it from the sticker
you've fixed to your orange hat:
Use first. I mean the head, all wit.
      May you?

VICTORY

for a trucking daughter,
and after Marianne Moore

The poet said it wouldn't
    come to her unless
    she went to it. Express

you've gone there, climbed
    the little ladder, perched
    behind the wheel to launch

all seventy-three feet
    of rubber, steel, and spark,
    explosive power. The ark

you keep keeps you between
    the lines except to pass
    inferiors, or cross

to other states. I see you
    in my rear-view mirror:
    each high-riding driver

of a live-in truck is maybe
    you, who once jumped horses,
    leaving me to parse

my fatal sentences outside the ring.
    You, who overcome
    the chemistry of harm,

the choker strung on DNA.
What is there like fortitude!
to clear this Julie's road.

DEFINITION: NORTHERN CALIFORNIA AUTUMN

To my grandson Logan

The flowers whose blooming I missed
this July when I walked Vermont beside
you tapping the walls of your mother
then knocking hard
before we all breathed the one
sunset over Lake Champlain
those flowers are blooming again, more profuse
for the cool nights, still more
sweet for hummingbirds whose choice
Mexican salvia raises high
purple torches to light
the shortening days

as your face slips further
beyond the stratosphere I traveled
home—where my house is—
to the place I call exile, far
from you who wear my maiden name.
Last night when I reached
you shrank, began to melt...
waking, in a green book I ranged
your photos, page after page enlarged you
restored your mouth whistling, sucking, singing hosannas
to your mama my child, now
someone new

tied to me by more than blood
commothers, matrifilipeers
let the language expand to record
our newborn relation

and joy to its maker, you
you buster, you redheaded you

THINKING BACK THROUGH MY
MOTHER: THE FARM, EARLY 1900s

For we think back through our mothers if we are women.
— Virginia Woolf

My teacher is patient and never yet
A lesson of hers did I once forget.
                    — Katherine Lee Bates,
          "Vacation Song" in Souvenir at Close of School
          School District No. 116
          Hayward Twp., Freeborn County, Minnesota
          May 29, 1919

I. LITTLE SISTER, THEIR GAME

All day a world of knees in my face: bony,
scabbed over where they dropped from trees.
Mama tells Art and Helen *Take care of Ann,*
I hear her, but as soon as we round
the curve in the dirt road, as soon
as the apple trees close behind us
they begin their game. *Wait . . . No*
I call while they giggle and stretch
their long legs over the road
in scissors steps and I am pumping
mine up and down up and down,
my face wrung like one of Mama's rags
as road, trees, field blur
and spill down my cheeks.

Then, because this is the game, they stop
and swing me between them like a pail
full of Bessie's milk and we're off
through the fields where the grass wall
waves and hums with crickets and bees
who make the rounds like the mail wagon
past our farm and Olaf's and Paddy's
only instead of delivering they're taking,
drinking the clover like sweets from a barrel.
If we could only see their purple chins.

Art and Helen hold me between them like that,
making a path so I won't go under this grass
the way Walter slipped into the flood
when ooph they let go and run in two directions,
all I can see around me is tall, green.
I'm lost in the hair of a giant's body
where sun can get through but I can't see the road
back to Mama and Papa, to my doll Sarah
who sits at the table guarding my chair
so Arthur can't have it. Where's the way up,
I'm sinking under grass
under the ground with all the worms
like Papa digs when he ploughs,
and the grass is growing on top of me.
Now Arthur and Helen will laugh because
they never have to take me along.

While I'm thinking this, ready
to scream what Mama calls *bloody murder*
so she'll come to find me and whip them,
a cool rope slides around my ankle

and I look down in time to see it write S, S
before getting lost in the grass too.
I take a deep breath, my voice lifts out
through the part in my hair, high and straight,
making the grass shake until I hear
the blades rub their hands together as those two
come threshing over before they get it from Mama.
Helen wipes my face with her shirt,
which comes away brown and wet.
Art pokes me in my most tickly rib,
and it isn't funny.

Don't think
you'll get away with this, you big bullies.
Just wait. I'm going to tell.

II. Photo, Me Trying Not To Fall

Ice and the cellar door's slant
pitch me down and sun makes my eyes tear
but I smile because Papa says so.
If the camera took feeling you'd scratch
your fingers on my chapped cheeks,
you'd frostbite them on my nose. The only
thing warm on my face is one pearl
that's just slid from a nostril.
In this white fur hat and coat—Papa's rabbits,
Mama's patterns and stitches—
I'm swell even though Helen wore it first.
They thought I'd never grow. Three weeks
old, with whooping cough, I got held on a pillow
like the king's crown. Look at me now, everyone,

look. I'm the princess in ermine. *Shoo!*
Papa, make Helen get out of my picture.

III. RUNNING AWAY WITH RALPH

Arthur kept pulling my braids
and it wasn't my fault.
Mama stood in the kitchen, canning
while the others all played that game
he said I couldn't nanh-nanh.
I shuffled away.
They didn't care.
Ralph was stretched beside the pump.
I pulled his big fan of a tail
and he turned to lick
my hand, ready to follow
me anywhere. I whispered
and we both slunk away.
We could go to Bohemia
that place Mrs. Brabec came from
with her raspberry cakatchys.
It was getting hot. I yawned.
We came to the toolshed, a hideout
with just enough space
to crawl under and still see
through the X's if Arthur
or strange devils walked by.
Ralph curled up and I leaned
my head on him for a furry pillow
all smooth since Mama cut
out the burrs. I sniffed
his own pure dog smell

hoping I smelled to him
like no other child.
We slept there till dusk
and never knew how Mama
thought we'd got drowned or lost.
Seventy years later
when they sliced my heart valve
I would wake
from that heavy sleep calling
Ralph . . .

IV. For Harold, 'Mighty In Battle'

You first Harold of my life
we wanted to learn together
what it meant that spring
your neighbor's foal died.
You got two pitchforks
and we started digging.
When yours slipped it aimed
straight for my eye.
That time I was lucky:
not blind, no scar.

The afternoon a long-tailed cloud
came flying like a big mad kite
toward us, we fell face-down,
held tight to cornstalks
and when the wind stopped
we got up, that field bent flat as glass.

Danger seemed to find and miss us.

When your sisters ran panting
to our door, almost beat it down
for Mama right away to help,
you were that sick, she dropped
her knitting, grabbed my hand
and from the road we heard you howl
before we saw you doubled over
on the floor. The two mothers
lifted you to the kitchen table,
kneaded hard your bellyful
to make you rise again.
Sun advanced across the boards—
our mothers heaved, took turns, looked
for signs, encouragement
before they finally cried.
How could you die of eating some green apples?
How could you go with that foal?

V. Pneumonia/Delirium: I Join The Worst County News

The dark shape framed in light
slices my chest with an ax, in/out
the girl who stayed home

> *hacked to pieces . . . robbery . . .*
> *a laborer . . . men in barns*
> *leaped for their axes*

I am a Hindu floating
on that smoky river
my face pouring

kerosene over her head
and set fire to it

Sand piled on me, crushing
I can't push it off
to turn over, reach
the dancers on the wall

fingers . . . bitten by the woman
on finding herself buried alive

The brook gargles onto its banks
Someone draws back the weights
and a snowball lands on my chest
a mouth opens, spills doctor words

rales . . . pectoriloquy
like lungs speaking to ribs

In our school play I am the Swedish maid
and have to be funny, laugh up
blood onto the white linen cloths

from that shack
the odor of stale meat
and green bones

Mama in the kitchen preserving
deer skulls, the jars sweating tears
for the sad one

she deliberately lay down
in the Wisconsin River

On the coach, I have the sleeper
while the cows and horses stand
in the last car
All the ice-covered trees
brush the train as we ride   ride   make no sound

Called Home
Harold Hackbart, 1911-1917

Papa, come fetch us in the storm
hurry, white blades are chopping your red beard
fill the sleigh with blankets
and tuck us in like dolls

VI. Little Sister, Her Out-Of-Body Flight

This time he'll get me, he yells as I rip the cap
off his head and race out the back door.
Now I am grown too, but the lightest, fleetest.
No big fish flopping around yet under my shirt.
No wadding or stains between my legs to slow me
down.
Now even his flashy muscles are no guarantee.
They're a wheelbarrow full of stones he has to haul.

Oh no you don't, he surges after
but I am already charging out
toward the scarecrow, the parked tractor,
my legs arms lungs rooting for me
Ann, Ann, Ann, run

I turn to look over my shoulder at him
closing the gap, his grin like a telephone wire
hung between big, sunburned ears, the message
Who do you think you are, sowbreath?
but I've gloated on his face a whisker too long

the sun's lamp runs out of oil
as field, barn, windmill drop
into the furry dark . . .

I don't feel my fingers, don't know how I got up
above myself who lies there beside the tractor
her head emptying its colors into the earth's

look, I'm a hummingbird without wheels
I wear dragonfly veil, my two blue eyebulbs
peer down from their stalks
                                    at unharvested fields

WOMEN NEAR SEA

after a painting by Paul Delvaux

Taking what's left of the sun
in high-necked, clinging dresses,

they look like each other
but do not recognize themselves.

They could be women of pleasure,
oddly prim as they wait by the houses.

Perhaps weather makes them sit so still
on parlor chairs outside the closed doors,

makes them not see or speak.
Perhaps they are wooden figures

all sprung on the hour, now stuck,
unable to get back inside the clocks.

The women's hands nest in their laps.
No salt wind bothers their hair,

their skirts long enough to hide everything.
Women could die in such heat in such dresses.

Behind a door someone is calling
Martha or *Mother* but she will not answer.

In the distance she swims with the others,
their fins parting the sea.

LADY'S WRITING DESK, CIRCA 1880

Matters of little consequence,
narrow, it says.
Please come to tea
The embroidered pillowslips match
Dear James, Since you left for Princeton . . .

The joiner was just taking orders,
we are often smaller. But
J. Austen at a lady's writing desk? M. Curie?

Relax, I tell myself.
Genius writes in the palm of its own hand,
writes on the world's lap, on the air.
Desks notwithstanding.

Still, something is ominous here.
This desk would thank any corner,
would never intrude
on the conversations of overstuffed chairs.
A hundred years later,
a child's business is too big to fit.

This desk made some man a fine wife.

SLEEPING DAUGHTER

> *"The daughter of Edward J. Martin, a Marinette ex-*
> *alderman, has awakened after sleeping nearly a week.*
> *During that time her slumber was wholly unbroken and*
> *the strongest efforts of her attendants failed to waken her.*
> *Physicians ascribe her strange condition to a sort of*
> *nervous prostration due in a measure to the death of her*
> *mother last summer and a fright she received . . . She is*
> *17 years old."*
> —1899 state records, quoted in Michael
> Lesy, *Wisconsin Death Trip*

With a noose around his heart
poor father wandered room to room
searching for her: an innocent man
sentenced to life.
I had the little ones to distract
from her absence. Music had fled.
Now the birds' anthems struck our ears
like the schoolmaster's whip
as another day dared begin.

After the children had left for school
I stood at the soapstone sink
and watched them get smaller,
colored confetti blowing across the snow.
And all at once the whole length of him
was against me, pressing so hard my breath
would not come, the last of it
gone out on my cry. I thought I was dreaming,
the snowfield erupted in black puffs
as I struggled to make sense.

His hands leapt like flames over parts of me
no one had ever touched, not since
I began to bleed. This could not be.
I wanted to roll back this day
like a huge boulder into the mouth of a bear's cave,
wanted to undo these moments outside time.
Help me, he moaned as I turned to face him
who had made me along with the woman
newly gone from us all. No!
my mind shouted but when I opened my mouth
no sound came out—like the lamb last spring
hanged on the barbed wire which meant to secure it.
Now I saw his face, eyes rolled back, lips hanging
like the idiot boy from Merrill. I saw logs float
down the river, saw the men hammering
fenceposts, saw their 4-pound sledge open a log
I saw Mrs. Lundgren the midwife catching John
from the swollen almond that split
between Mother's thighs—all this I saw
in that instant when Papa clamped me
as for the worst thrashing. My knees unlocked
and the kitchen rose as I sank through the floorboards
down into the dirt cellar with stored grain,
rats, and in my nose held the stench of things
sodden and decayed, I fell further down
through the floor of that cellar
as earth resumed its shape over me
—I had never walked there—and the worm sang
and the beetle clicked, hidden in that deeper black
where I fell towards Mother.

And when I stopped at the core, packed into darkness
I felt the weight of a house on my chest, heard bones
splinter like teacups against a wall
I lay self-contained as a stone, mindless of day and night
until before me a silver thread shone, a snail's map
and I grasped it, pulled myself hand over slippery hand
to reach the lid of earth
where her voice prayed me Laura! climb back.

Opening my eyes,
I could not tell the distance of objects
nor whose bed, curtains, basin surrounded me.
Who were these men, pencils in hand, writing
as I blinked and moved my lips to speak
letting out a sound like a jail door opened slowly
against great resistance. I could not feel
where was my body.
Could as easily have lifted a barn ridgepole
as my arm which drew a white line
down the quilt, ended in a cluster of cornsilk.
Who was this man whose eyes pinned my face,
whose tangled beard hung past
the third button of his faded shirt?
I spat my rusty word, and woke again.

EVOLUTION DREAM

We stood at the bottom of the clay pit
steep sides rising all around
a bottleneck of sky shining straight
overhead, at our feet the bubbling
lagoon like sewage overturned
the bowl of my stomach
                    you said *we're all soup*
and I answered *I've been soup—*
I'm splitting—so I wheeled
to look for a way up
the ground crawled beneath me
ants, roaches, waterbugs, lizards
and enlarged variations
all up the sides of the pit, movement
superseding itself, bodies hierarchical
wavering on the slimy walls
                    when I found the stair in the rock
you'd already scaled it and I had to alone
trying not to feel the . . . the crawlers
all their legs striving so
I got to the top, looked over the night
a full moon shone on the ocean
calm as far as I could see,
to the finale, colored with royal
iridescence rich as oil slick
                    and you stood beside me
you touched me and
my hair turned white,
my understanding complete.

AT NIGHTFALL IN VERMONT

I head for the graveyard, away
from the house with yellow windows.
The mist hangs like intentions.
I'm in it when you stop me,

flying too hard to be birds
you flappers, you
loose-jointed gloves,
children of the night.

How Bela loved his at the stone casement!

Why should I fear?
Like you, I was kissed off
into darkness. I'd suck my thumb
as the room filled with vapors.
Hands, eyes inside. No big voices helped

the way the trees help you, talking
            psst, little whistles . . .
you just miss the irreversible each time.
People do this. We call them batty.
Was I?—then, and then?

Hairy brothers, you sleep all day
upside-down letting dreams
fall into the world. Now, flying,
you sing to see where you are.

THE MAMMOGRAM

Remove your shirt and bra, but
Do Not Remove the latest *Good Housekeeping*
from the examining room where the gaping
machine awaits your submission, lusts
for your breasts, those targets of various thirsts
—the Moroccan's *Pourquoi tu n'enlèves ça?*
(that gold hair which exclaimed *areola)*
—the American's *Why not silicone breast
augmentation?* Shall you spotlight his
undescended testicle? Place his spout unshriven
between plastic jaws, tell him
Hold your breath as the technician says,
serving your breasts for crêpes. And you'll
hold it all right, stopper your arias
of lamentation before the stacked, vigorous
woman who's cruel to sisters with a smile.
*Dear Doctor Joyce: Do they know
if such torturing diagnostic tools
cause damage? Mother said girls
shouldn't get punched there, lumps could grow.
I am writing this from my warm bath
with a green washcloth calming my breasts
where today's smothering test
still throbs. Doctor, please tell the truth.*
While the switch-thrower checks the plates
to be sure she got the right angles on you,
you leaf through *Good's* shiny pages, stew
in answers simple as toothpaste.
It's all a matter of big enough numbers—

12 Ways to Defuse Tension, 15 Country
Casseroles, 5 Tips for Gorgeous Gray
Hair, 14 Instant Beauty Changes This Year—
among which: *Shout, Close your eyes, Wear red.*
If only you get the numbers right, you'll keep
love, looks. Your two breasts, you hope
mammogram mirabilis will abide.
They've gone everywhere with you, new worlds
in Hygiene, onstage, senior prom,
the Croissant Rouge, Boston Science Museum,
your father's funeral, district court, Land's End.
The hungry ones who drained only your breasts
were two infants filled, consoled at them:
first fountains of antibodies, home
with fires stoked for the displaced.
Open your eyes. Still there. *Not
yet wearing red over your heart.*
O shout, you twin sisters,
helps to those who love without spite.

OLD WARS

I. The Should She Song

When a man tells a woman they're peers
because they don't have sex

is he treating her
like one of the boys

and should she take it like a man? :

Just what I've always thought, J.B. . . .
Jimbo, how about those Knicks?

or, should she take it like a woman,
shake it and break it to him like a woman—

Sex or no sex, honey. You're in arrears.

II. Our Hero, Revised

Then he came wearing a nimbus of long-
stemmed ideals and playing the flutesong
we wanted to follow into a black-and-white
dawn like Charlie Chaplin with Paulette.

Now biographers turn up puffs
of him: hand on an actress's rosy nipple,
legs spread beneath a roulette table,
mouth swapping calories with someone's wife.

How dared he shine like a substation,
a cure or world-class religious faith?
Hey, that light was ours we shone on him.
We built the tabernacle, burned the flame.

III. Storm Doors Cosmology

All night the heater paraded
beating drums, crashing cymbals.
Time to take summer down,
stop letting cold through the cracks
where doors hung uneven, parted
just where they should have formed one.
Next morning I searched for tools,
dragged storm doors from the rented garage.
First put them on upside-down, then inside-out,
then the whole door would swing shut
just as I fit glass in place,
would slip, twist, and my grip fail.
Sweat poured down my neck,
it was getting hot—maybe too hot for storm doors—
rust on one screw had worn down the threads
so I angled, pushed, pushed harder. Nothing held.
Baseball size bruises rose on my calf where
I'd fielded the weight of protection.
When myself I had to install it
oh how heavy the universe grew.

IV. Epilogue/ Sleeping Where You Sleep

You say you sleep all over the bed
well I do too, sailing
out for treasure or plunder
out to bury my dead fathoms down
where the schools of fish
form a handkerchief-waving cortège

and when the day wakes
so many birds announce our good news
I can't name or quote them
but they're all up for singing
each throat a pulse that thanks back
the pulse of the day

NOTE

Some of the italicized passages in "Pneumonia/Delirium: I Join the Worst County News" are quoted from newspaper and state records as reprinted in Michael Lesy's *Wisconsin Death Trip* (New York: Doubleday, 1973).